How To Catch Crabs

A Pacific Coast Guide

Charlie White

National Library of Canada Cataloguing in Publication Data

White, Charles, 1925-
How to Catch Crabs

ISBN 1-895811-51-1   Softcover

1. Crabbing—Pacific Coast (B.C.)
2. Crabbing—Pacific Coast (U.S.)
I. Title

SH400.5.C7W49 1998   799.2'55386   C98-910128-2

First edition: 1970
Second edition: 1998   Reprinted: 2003

Heritage House acknowledges the financial support for our publishing program from the Government of Canada through the Book Publishing Industry Development Program (BPIDP), Canada Council for the Arts, and the British Columbia Arts Council.

Cover design and typesetting: Darlene Nickull
Original artwork: Nelson Dewey
Cover photos: Front, Rodger Touchie; back, Robert H. Jones

HERITAGE HOUSE PUBLISHING COMPANY LTD.
Unit #108 - 17665 66A Ave., Surrey, BC V3S 2A7

Printed in Canada

BRITISH
COLUMBIA
ARTS COUNCIL
We acknowledge the support of the Province of British Columbia through the British Columbia Arts Council

The Canada Council | Le Conseil des Arts
for the Arts | du Canada

Contents

Acknowledgements

Grateful thanks are extended to all who helped in preparation of this book. Special thanks to Mr. T.H. Butler of the Fisheries Research Board of Canada, Mr. Dale Snow of the Oregon Fish Commission, to the Washington State Department of Fisheries, and to Mr. Walter Norbury of Sidney, B.C.

We are grateful for the special permission granted by Mr. Butler to use material from his study of crabs and crab traps in conjunction with an underwater TV camera.

Always check current regulations, restrictions,
and regional closings with local officials.

Foreword

Over the past three decades, Charlie White has proven to be one of the West Coast's most prolific and popular marine and fishing writers.

Charlie's writings, innovations, inventions, product designs and research have kept him at the forefront of marine technology. A tribute to his keen eye is the fact that some of his books written almost thirty years ago remain timely and of great practical use today.

After more than 100,000 copies and eleven printings of *How to Catch Crabs,* this new edition reflecting our environmental times, current catch regulations and Charlie's latest techniques seems overdue.

Like Charlie's words, illustrator Nelson Dewey's drawings retain their relevance and add humour to a process that can be both fun and rewarding.

As Charlie says with every printing, "It is difficult to believe that there are so many persons interested in catching crabs."

Types Of Edible Crabs

Cancer magister

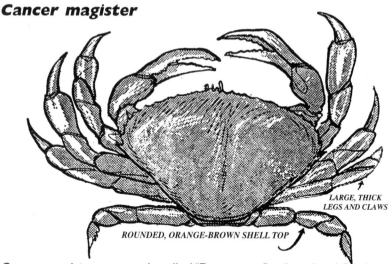

LARGE, THICK
LEGS AND CLAWS

ROUNDED, ORANGE-BROWN SHELL TOP

Cancer magister, commonly called "Dungeness" or "sand crab," is the major commercial crab found in the Pacific Northwest and British Columbia. The males grow to eight to ten inches (twenty to twenty-five centimetres) across the back (carapace). They have large meaty legs and claws plus a large knot of body meat in the muscular portion of the body immediately adjoining the legs.

Cancer productus

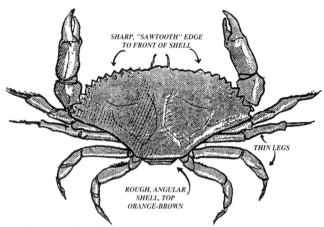

SHARP, "SAWTOOTH" EDGE
TO FRONT OF SHELL

THIN LEGS

ROUGH, ANGULAR
SHELL, TOP
ORANGE-BROWN

Cancer productus, or "rock crab," is not caught commercially, but has quite edible meat. Rock crabs are smaller than Dungeness and have harder, reddish-brown shells. They have large strong claws, but their legs are small and spindly, with little meat. The body also contains little meat, but if you have patience it is possible to get a nice meal from rock crabs.

Box crabs

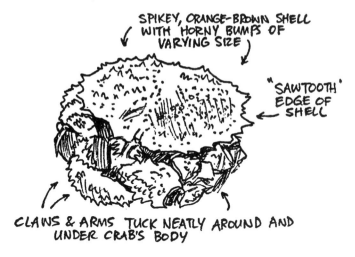

SPIKEY, ORANGE-BROWN SHELL
WITH HORNY BUMPS OF
VARYING SIZE

"SAWTOOTH"
EDGE OF
SHELL

CLAWS & ARMS TUCK NEATLY AROUND AND
UNDER CRAB'S BODY

There are two subspecies of box crabs. They are quite edible but are seldom taken by sport crabbers. Instead these deep-water crabs are usually captured by scuba divers on rocky bottoms.

Some larger specimens are called king crabs, but this is not the same species as the much larger Alaskan variety.

King crabs

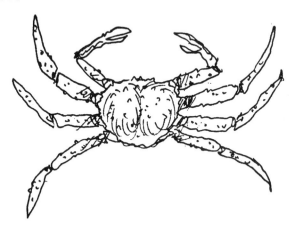

These huge and very tasty crustaceans are fished primarily in deep water off the coast of Alaska. Local populations have also been found in the northern inlets along the B.C. coast and in the Queen Charlotte Islands. They have also been found in the Prince Rupert area and in Grenville Channel.

We have no information of any sport fishing being done for these giants, but it might be an exciting adventure to go on an expedition for them.

Finding Likely Locations For Crabs

The easiest and most reliable method of finding local crab populations is to ask questions of the residents of the area. Marinas, tackle shops, boat rentals and similar commercial establishments can usually advise of the best crabbing spots.

Look for crab traps on board other boats at marinas or in boat harbours and ask the occupants where they catch their crabs. Most will be very helpful.

Generally, the Dungeness crab can be found on a sandy bottom where there is a good tidal movement. Along Oregon, Washington and the west coast of Vancouver Island, the commercial crabbers get the majority of their catches in the open sea off shore using large, heavy commercial traps. The sport crabber will usually find it more practical to fish in small bays and especially in river mouths and estuaries.

In the inland waters of Puget Sound and the Strait of Georgia, look for a sandy bottom with eel grass or a sandy bottom at the mouth of a river or stream. Good crab catches are often made off a long sand spit.

Rock crabs are widely distributed throughout the inland waters and can be found in almost any type of bottom (rock, gravel or sand).

Jurisdiction over sport fishing along the west coast of North America is controlled by the Canadian and B.C. governments and by individual American states. Do not go crabbing or fishing without checking current government regulations.

The *B.C. Tidal Waters Sport Fishing Guide*, published annually by Fisheries and Oceans Canada, is available free of charge at sporting-goods stores, marinas, and similar outlets. The guide contains all current regulations governing sport fishing for salmon, halibut, rockfish, crabs, oysters, and other species.

For information on Alaska, Washington, Oregon, and California, refer to page 62, which lists websites that contain current sport-fishing regulations.

Crabbing Calendar

Crabs may be taken any time of the year in many areas, but individual populations migrate short distances so the crabs might disappear from any particular area at certain times. Adult male crabs tend to migrate from deep to shallow water during the spring and early summer. This seems especially true in open coastal areas.

Crabs are generally available in coastal bays at any time of the year except when heavy rainfall and strong flowing rivers lower the salinity in the bays. This forces the crabs into the saltier water outside the bay.

Is There A Best Season For Crabs?

In British Columbia, crabs can be taken at any time of the year. They are also available on the Oregon and Washington coasts most of the year, but there are closed seasons in certain areas. Be sure to check your local regulations before embarking on a crabbing expedition.

Crabs are in their best condition when the shell is firm and hard and when the crab feels heavy.

Soft shelled crabs and lightweight, "empty feeling" crabs are not as desirable. A short description of the moulting habits of crabs will help explain the reasons for this.

Crabs have a hard exoskeleton (outer shell) covering their entire body and legs. This shell is fixed in size and the crab can grow only by shedding its shell and growing a new and larger one. This process is called "moulting."

The young crab moults six or seven times during the first years of life, with less frequent moultings as it grows larger. Crabs reach a size of about 1 3/4 inches (4 1/2 centimetres) across the back of the shell in the first year and four inches (ten centimetres) after two years. Male crabs reach 5 3/4 to 6 inches (14 1/2 to 15 1/4 centimetres) after three years. At this point they are sexually mature.

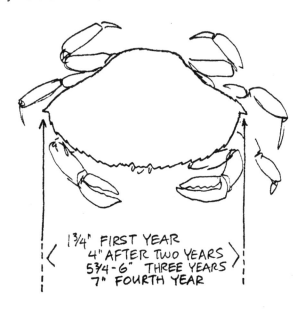

1¾" FIRST YEAR
4" AFTER TWO YEARS
5¾-6" THREE YEARS
7" FOURTH YEAR

Fourth-Year Moult

... ARE YOU GONNA... DO IT...NOW?

In the fourth year the crab moults again and increases its body weight approximately 50 percent and its shell width to about seven inches (eighteen centimetres) or slightly less. Most commercially caught crabs are in this size range and are in their fourth year of life. This allows the male crab to mate once before reaching legal size.

(MOULTING
  SPLIT)

When the crab is ready to shed its shell, a split appears across the rear of the shell and allows the crab (with a butter-soft new skin) to literally back out of his old shell. He leaves behind a complete shell including back, legs and claws.

Most moulting occurs in May and June although it can take place at any time of the year. When there is a large population of moulting crabs, the fisheries department often gets calls from alarmed seaside residents reporting thousands of dead crabs on the beach. The "dead crabs" are the empty moulted shells.

After moulting, the crab immediately absorbs water and swells up to its new larger size, protected only by its soft skin. Usually it will bury itself in the sand for several days until the skin begins to harden into a new shell. Then it will come out of the sand and feed ravenously in order to fill its newly enlarged body with meat.

Soft Shells

Crabs caught during this period have soft shells and not much meat in them. The body meat tastes as good as ever (although there is much less of it), but the leg and claw meat seems to be a bit stringy and a little bit mushy.

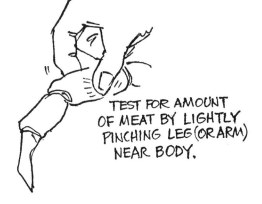

TEST FOR AMOUNT OF MEAT BY LIGHTLY PINCHING LEG (OR ARM) NEAR BODY.

It takes from thirty to sixty days for the shell to completely harden and the crab to become heavy and solid again.

Moulting formerly posed special problems for fisheries research personnel. Long-term crab studies were difficult because tagged crabs would shed their shells each season. This problem was solved by using a special tag that was placed along the "splitting line" and sewed into the flesh with a surgical needle. Now the tag goes along with the crab when it moults, making long-term tagging experiments practical.

Methods Of Capture

There are several popular methods of capturing crabs.

By Hand Or Scooping

The most exciting way to catch crabs is by hand, since you must stalk and capture them on the run. In bays, estuaries and inland waters the method for boaters is to drift slowly over shallow areas with eel grass and a sandy bottom at low tide and the early stages of a flooding tide. Waders can be equally as successful slowly moving through the shallows with a keen eye and a pair of gloves.

When you spot a crab moving along the bottom, scoop it into the boat with a longhandled crab scoop (see illustration). A fish landing net can also be used. Some persons use a garden rake, but this is undesirable because you will injure or kill the crab and will not be able to return females and undersized crabs to the water. In many areas it is also illegal. I discourage the use of spears and other pointed objects for the same reason —and in most areas spearing is illegal.

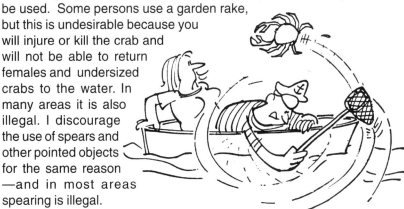

Hand crabbing is often done in late spring when the male and female crabs are together in shallow water in "mating pairs." While the act of mating takes a half hour or less, the male will often carry the female clasped to his underside for a month or more, waiting for her to moult, since this is the only time when successful mating can take place.

If you see crabs in such mating pairs, the male will almost certainly be a solid specimen in top condition. He will sometimes drop the female during the chase but if not, you can always release her after capture.

Along open coastal areas, you can capture crabs by wading through potholes or other tidal pools left by the receding tide. Wear hip or waist waders and tie a burlap sack or large plastic bucket around the waist. This will hold the crabs and leave both hands and the body free for active pursuit.

Crabs can often be found buried in the sand or hiding under seaweed or other debris. Capture them by kicking them out into the open or prodding them out with a stick.

Crab Rings

Crab rings are very popular along the Oregon and Washington coast. They are used primarily in river mouths and protected bays, but it is possible to use crab rings off the open shoreline on calm days. Always check local regulations for seasonal restrictions.

A crab ring is a simple but ingenious piece of equipment. Two wire rings form the top and bottom of a collapsible basket, the lower ring smaller than the upper, with strong netting forming the sides. Heavy chicken wire, cotton webbing or other suitable materials are used for the bottom.

After the bait is tied securely to the bottom of the basket, lower the basket to the bay bottom where the sides collapse and the top and bottom rings lie together, leaving only a flat platform of tempting bait that the crab can easily reach. After the ring has been left on the bottom for a length of time, raise it rapidly by pulling a rope which is attached to the sides of the top ring. This pulls up the sides of the basket and prevents the crabs from escaping while the basket is pulled into the boat.

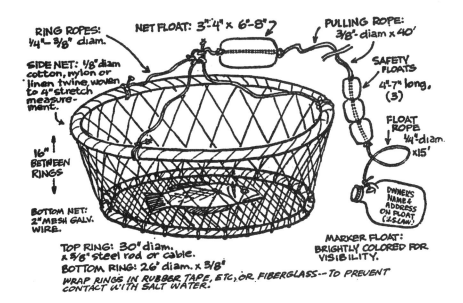

RING ROPES: ¼"—⅜" diam.

NET FLOAT: 3"-4" x 6"-8"

PULLING ROPE: ⅜"- diam x 40'

SIDE NET: ⅛" diam cotton, nylon or linen twine, woven to 4" stretch measurement.

SAFETY FLOATS 4"-7" long, (3)

FLOAT ROPE ¼" diam. x15'

16" BETWEEN RINGS

OWNER'S NAME & ADDRESS ON FLOAT (2 S.LAW)

BOTTOM NET: 2" MESH GALV. WIRE.

MARKER FLOAT: BRIGHTLY COLORED FOR VISIBILITY.

TOP RING: 30" diam. x ⅝" steel rod or cable.
BOTTOM RING: 26" diam. x ⅜"
WRAP RINGS IN RUBBER TAPE, ETC, OR FIBERGLASS -- TO PREVENT CONTACT WITH SALT WATER.

In areas where crabs are plentiful, crab rings should be pulled every fifteen or twenty minutes if they are set in water too deep to see the bottom. Otherwise the crabs will steal the bait and leave.

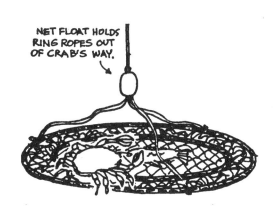

NET FLOAT HOLDS RING ROPES OUT OF CRAB'S WAY.

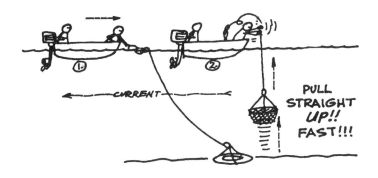

CURRENT

PULL STRAIGHT UP!! FAST!!!

Crab Traps

This is often the easiest and most efficient method of catching crabs, but it is also the most expensive. Crab traps can cost from $25 for a collapsible model to $150 or more for the stainless steel trap.

Crab traps come in all shapes and sizes and most of them will catch some crabs under the right conditions. However, commercial crabbers who must get the maximum number of crabs possible in order to make a living, all tend to use a trap of the general design illustrated below. This type of trap has the following features that appear to make it more effective.

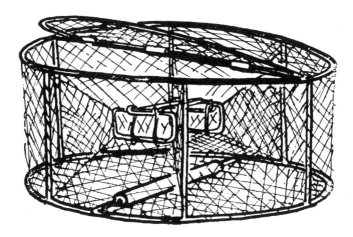

Rounded top and bottom rings - A hungry crab on the move sometimes does not go around the sharp corners on square or rectangular traps. It will just keep on going in the same direction when he comes to a sharp corner. Therefore, a round-sided trap allows the crab to work its way around to the entrance tunnels.

Side entrance tunnels - Entrance tunnels should be on the rounded sides of the trap rather than on the top for the same reason as listed above. A crab may have difficulty getting around a sharp corner between the side and top of the trap. The round trap tends to overcome this problem.

A crab's natural tendency upon arriving at the trap is to work its way around the side trying to get in rather than climbing over the top. Two entrance tunnels are usually sufficient, although four entrance tunnels make it easier for the crab to gain entrance. Four entrance tunnels require a huge trap and this is usually impractical for the sport crabber.

Anti-escape hinge - This is simply one or two pieces of wire hanging from the top of the inner end of the entrance tunnel. The crab pushes the hinge out of the way when it enters the trap. Then the hinge falls back into place, preventing the crab from escaping through the entrance tunnel.

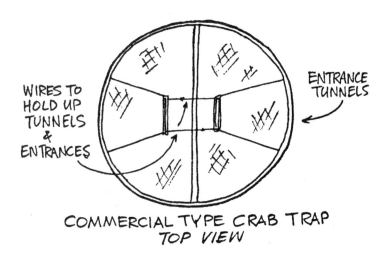

WIRES TO HOLD UP TUNNELS & ENTRANCES

ENTRANCE TUNNELS

COMMERCIAL TYPE CRAB TRAP
TOP VIEW

Long entrance tunnel - These make it more difficult for the crab to escape.

Several years ago I began using large commercial-sized stainless steel traps with an escape hole for undersize crabs. I think this is a good idea, especially on longer sets. The smaller crabs can find their way out, which saves you the trouble of taking them out of the trap. It also tends to save the bait to attract more big ones! As a conservation measure, the small males and females who escape are not subject to fighting and damage by other crabs in the trap.

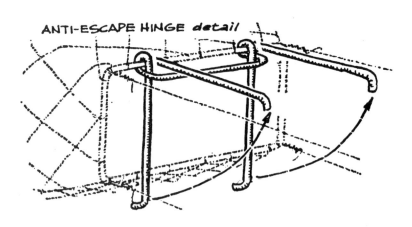

ANTI-ESCAPE HINGE *detail*

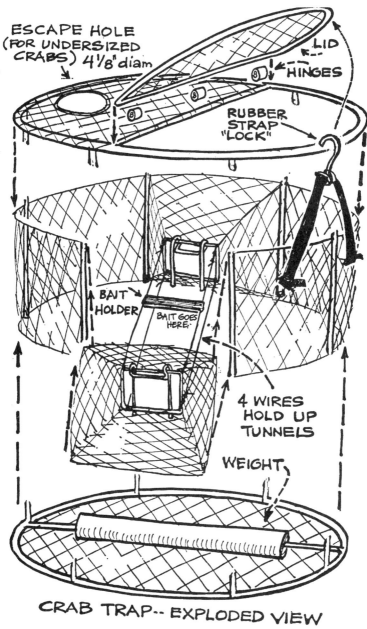

ESCAPE HOLE
(FOR UNDERSIZED
CRABS) 4⅛" diam

LID

HINGES

RUBBER
STRAP
"LOCK"

BAIT
HOLDER

BAIT GOES
HERE.

4 WIRES
HOLD UP
TUNNELS

WEIGHT

CRAB TRAP-- EXPLODED VIEW

Wire Vs Fabric

There is much debate about whether to use metal wire or fabric netting to construct traps. While some feel that crabs prefer fabric net, most commercial crabbers use stainless steel wire and find it works extremely well.

Collapsible Traps

Collapsible crab traps are easy to store on board a boat or in a car and can be reasonably effective traps. They are most effective when set for a few hours only as the crabs tend to escape when the trap is left overnight or longer.

Choosing A Sport Model Crab Trap

I have been experimenting with many different shapes and sizes of crab traps in an attempt to come up with the best compromise for the sport crabber. In all of my tests I have used the standard commercial stainless steel trap described on the preceding pages as a control trap to measure the relative effectiveness of my test models. The stainless trap, especially the forty-inch (102 centimetre) diameter model with rounded sides, long entrance tunnel and anti-escape hinge, has invariably outfished any other design.

There are several promising designs, however, which are less expensive to manufacture and have other advantages for the casual, weekend crabber. The large stainless steel commercial models are now selling for up to $150

each, plus the cost of line, floats, bait cup, etc. This is really too large an investment for many weekend crabbers.

In addition to keeping costs down, we wanted a trap that was easy to bait, allowed easy removal of the catch and stood up well to salt-water corrosion. We have learned that a B.C. firm, Sak Industries of Richmond, makes lightweight crab and prawn traps. They are collapsible and appear to be corrosion resistant. Similar products are no doubt available in the coastal states. Check with your local sporting goods store.

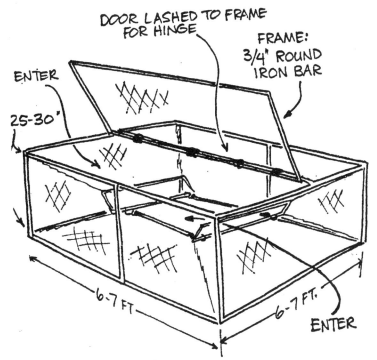

COVERING: NYLON NET OR WIRE MESH.

NYLON: TOP, SIDES & BOTTOM, 9½" STRETCHED MESH, 10/72 THREAD. TUNNEL, 3½" 10/72 NET.

KING CRAB TRAP DETAILS

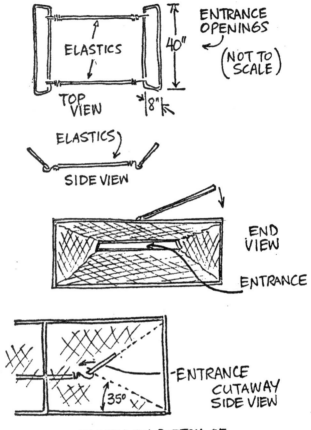

ENTRANCE OPENINGS

$\left(\substack{NOT\ TO \\ SCALE}\right)$

ELASTICS

40"

TOP VIEW

8"

ELASTICS

SIDE VIEW

END VIEW

ENTRANCE

ENTRANCE CUTAWAY SIDE VIEW

35°

ELASTIC ON BOTTOM OF ENTRANCES PULLS THEM TOGETHER, HOLDS ENTRY RAMP AT PROPER ANGLE.

Crab Baits

Contrary to popular belief, crabs are not scavengers and will not generally eat putrefied spoiled bait. They much prefer fresh food (the fresher the better) and live in nature on clams, marine worms, and small fish. One researcher in Oregon has found that old or smelly baits tend to catch undersize males and females while the larger males seek fresher food. (This is probably due to the old law of nature about survival of the fittest. The smaller crabs have greater difficulty competing for the freshest food so they sometimes will accept the less desirable spoiled food.)

Clams are generally considered the most effective bait for crabs, but my own experience shows that fresh salmon carcasses and entrails are hard to beat. Any fresh flesh or entrails from any marine animal should make an effective crab bait.

On days when crabs are plentiful and coming well to the traps, I have experimented with various types of bait. On one occasion I placed a variety of half a dozen different types of bait in the traps and pulled them within half an hour to see which baits the crabs ate first. To my surprise I found that the crabs seemed to prefer salmon eggs to anything else! In every instance where salmon eggs were available in the trap, **every crab** in the trap had a salmon egg in its mouth. (However, salmon eggs are most difficult to keep in a trap for any length of time.)

Non-Marine Baits

I have experimented using meat from non-marine animals. Table scraps of beef and pork were placed in traps near others containing conventional baits. In every case, the traps containing the beef or pork scraps were empty while the others had a good catch. While this experiment is not conclusive, it suggests that flesh of non-marine creatures is not good crab bait.

Squid, Octopus, Clams

Frozen squid is a popular bait with commercial crabbers on the B.C. coast. This may be because it is easily available. Other crabbers feel that oily fish like herring are very effective. I have had some excellent catches using herring .

Even octopus meat has been used as crab bait. However, the octopus is the mortal enemy of the crab and when whole chunks of octopus were placed in the traps, the crabs would not come near it. If the octopus meat was skinned, it looked like any other white bait and the crabs devoured it without realizing it was the flesh of their feared predator.

Large butter clams make excellent crab bait if you break them up before placing them in the bait jar. When I am digging clams I keep the littlenecks and small butter clams for steaming or clam chowder. The large butter clams, usually found deeper in the sand, are saved for crab bait.

When using clams, mussels, fish entrails or other soft bait, you can place it in potato or onion sacks or in a bag made from herring or shrimp nets. You can also use small-mesh chicken wire to make a cage. These makeshift containers can be lashed closed with heavy string. Make sure, however, to leave enough extra string to tie the container into the trap. (During our tests we worked with Scott Plastics in Victoria, B.C., to develop a proper bait jar that was subsequently called "Crab Diner." Check your local sporting goods store and if it is not available, phone Scott Plastics.)

Frozen Bait

If you have room in the freezer (and can talk your wife into letting you use it) crab bait can be prepared and frozen ahead of time.

After a successful fishing trip I clean my salmon, cod, etc. and then filet the meat for cooking. This leaves the head, tail, entrails, and the main backbone with attached smaller bones.

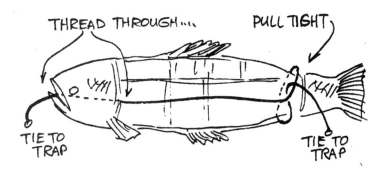

Using a stove pipe wire or any malleable wire (or even nylon line), wire these parts together before freezing. (If you try to wire up the bait after removing it from the freezer, you will need an electric drill to get through the frozen flesh!) Next, wrap the bait in newspaper or a plastic bag and place in the freezer. Clams can be placed in plastic bags, without water, and then broken apart and placed in bait jars after removal from the freezer.

This takes up some valuable space in the freezer, but it assures a ready supply of fresh crab bait when the crabbing opportunity arises. Many times, especially in the winter months, it is the only way to have fresh bait on hand for that day when the sun comes out and you want to go fishing and crabbing on short notice.

Freezing crab bait also offers the advantage of a slow and continuous release of the bait smell as the current slowly thaws the bait.

"Frozen Crabber"

A delightful winter outing starts with setting the crab traps, followed by two or three hours of fishing winter Chinooks, then returning to the traps before coming home. Quite often I return with a nice salmon or two and a good catch of crabs in prime condition.

Placing The Bait

All crab baits should be wired or tied securely in the centre of the trap between the entrance tunnels. If baits are just thrown loose into the traps, they will drift to one corner and the crabs will feed on them from the outside. Placing the bait between the entrance tunnels encourages the crab to enter the trap.

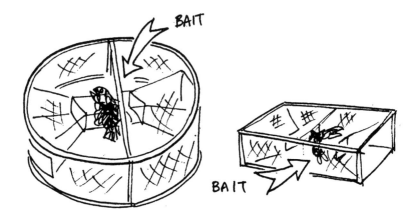

When using soft baits or small pieces (clams, fish eggs, etc.), you should place them in a plastic or metal container with holes punched in it. This will allow the smell to get out into the water without allowing the bait to drift away. This container should be wired in place between the entrance tunnels. You can make your own or use the bait jar described earlier.

Setting The Trap

Choose a spot off a sandy shore in fifteen to forty feet (four to twelve metres) of water with good tidal movement. Eel grass in the shallow water is also a good sign. If there are floats of other crab traps, it is probably a good bet to set yours in the same general vicinity. This assumes that the person setting the trap before you had some local knowledge. If the other crabbers were also strangers in the area, you may all end up in the wrong place!

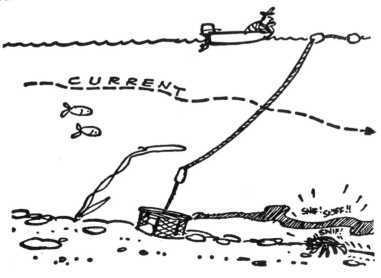

If you cannot tell the character of the bottom, you can usually find information on marine charts that list (with a symbol) whether the bottom is sand, mud, or rock.

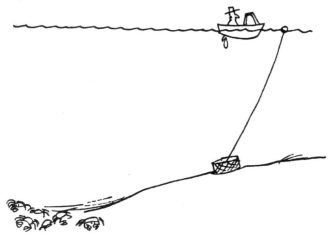

Setting traps in deeper water can also be productive, but the great majority of crabs taken from in-shore waters (both commercial and sport) are taken in less than sixty feet (eighteen metres) of water. If you have been successful catching crabs in a certain area and they have disappeared, it may be that they have moved into the adjacent deeper water. In this instance you might try setting your trap down to 100 feet (thirty metres) or more.

Line Up Tunnel Entrances

The Pacific Biological Station in Nanaimo, B.C., conducted some interesting experiments in the Queen Charlotte Islands to determine how crabs approached and entered a trap. PBS also analysed the behaviour of crabs inside the trap. They used an underwater TV camera mounted on a tripod above the trap and observed the crabs as they came into the field of view.

1) In practically all cases, the crabs approached the trap against the current, almost always in direct line with the current. This indicates that the crabs were picking up the smell of the bait and following it directly to the trap itself.

2) When the tunnel entrance was lined up with the current flow, the crabs would often walk directly up the tunnel and into the trap. If the tunnels were set at 90 degrees to the tidal flow, the crabs would often walk back and forth outside the trap and sometimes claw at the trap mesh. Some crabs would work their way around to the tunnel entrance but others would just wander off.

This interesting experiment taught me to be very careful in lining the tunnel entrances with the tidal flow when setting a crab trap. If the tunnel entrances are lined up with the tidal flow and the trap is dropped with a slack line, it will usually land on the bottom with the tunnels properly aligned.

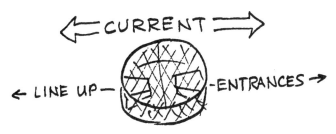

If you are setting the trap in strange waters, be sure to check the depth before setting the trap. If you do not have a depth sounder, you can measure with a piece of fishing line with weight attached.

You can also just hold on to the marker float until you are sure the trap landed on the bottom. If these precautions are not followed, you may see your float disappear under water, the trap gone forever as it sinks into water deeper than your float line.

When fishing multiple traps (or crab rings), it is a good idea to place them seventy-five to a hundred feet (twenty-three to thirty metres) apart. If you have a number of likely spots to cover, you can of course spread the traps over a much wider area. If crabbing near a boat channel (as in the harbours and inlets on the Oregon and Washington coasts), it is a good idea to place the floats parallel to the channel and not across it. This will lessen the likelihood of a boat tangling with your float line.

Marking The Spot

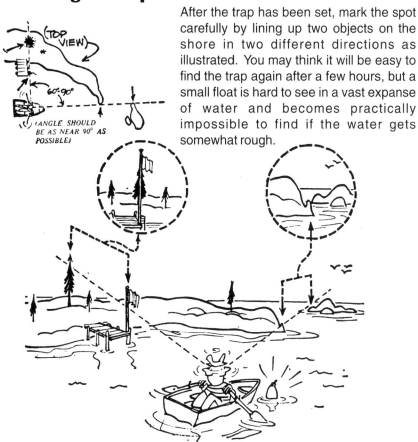

After the trap has been set, mark the spot carefully by lining up two objects on the shore in two different directions as illustrated. You may think it will be easy to find the trap again after a few hours, but a small float is hard to see in a vast expanse of water and becomes practically impossible to find if the water gets somewhat rough.

Best Times For Crabbing

I always felt that crabs fed only on a flooding tide and only set my traps at these times. However, my experiences over the last couple of years and information from fisheries department sources have changed my thinking.

Crabs do feed better on a flooding tide than on an ebbing tide of the same magnitude. However, crabs seem to feed best at slack tide or when there is very little tidal movement. When you think about it, this is the time when the crabs have the least current resistance to overcome and are more free to move about in search of food.

I would rate the times for catching crabs in the following order:

Best
Just prior to and during high slack tide.
Low slack tide and immediately following.
Good
During a small flood tide.
Fair
During a small ebb tide.
Poor
During a fast-flowing flood tide.
Yecchhh!
During a fast-flowing ebb tide.

When To Pull The Trap

Traps may be pulled and checked every two hours or they may be left for long periods. Pulling the trap frequently has the advantage of letting you know whether you are in a productive spot and also allows you to remove small crabs, starfish and other predators who devour the bait.

Leaving the trap for longer periods, on the other hand, can allow more crabs to find their way into the trap. There may be a number of crabs just approaching or trying to find the tunnel entrance when you pull the trap to check it. When you drop trap again, it may be dozens of feet away and crabs have to start finding it all over again.

Float Line Problems

Strong tidal currents will often pull the marker float completely underwater. Even a large float can sometimes be pulled under in a strong tidal surge. If using a bleach bottle or other plastic jug for a float, be sure it is tightly secured to the line.

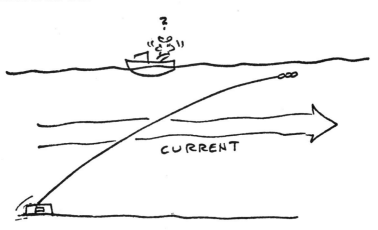

If you are using bleach bottles, try dipping the metal caps into some kind of waterproofing material (paint or liquid rubber for instance) after you've screwed them tightly onto the bottles. Nothing's more infuriating than to lose a trap because the cap rusted through and the float bottle sank.

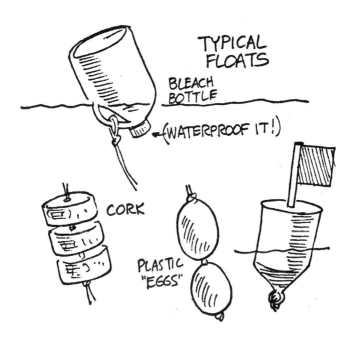

If your floats are pulled under and you wish to correct the situation without changing to larger floats, you can simply add ten feet (three metres) of line from your existing float to a smaller float. This smaller float will then act as a marker to allow you to retrieve the main float.

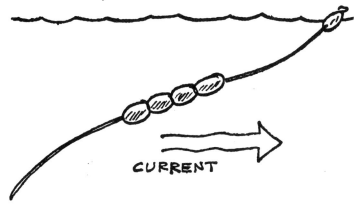

Sometimes it is desirable to have the crab traps remain under water at all tides. If the traps are set in an area of heavy boat traffic or where trap piracy is a problem, you can use the method illustrated.

When setting traps in this manner, it is extremely important to take accurate shore markings using the gunsight (or "ranging") method of lining up one object behind another. The trap line is retrieved by dragging a grappling line behind the boat along the gunsight marks previously established.

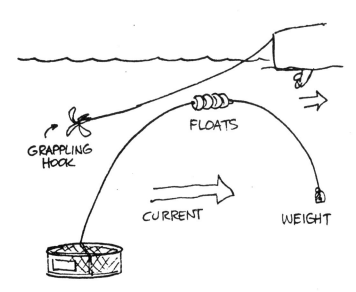

If you start catching rock crabs, you are probably over a rocky area and Dungeness crab will be scarce. This can sometimes be misleading (I have sometimes caught rock crabs along with Dungeness in my favourite crabbing hole), but it is usually a pretty good sign that you are in the wrong place.

As crabs mature they often segregate themselves according to size and sex. The males will sometimes be found at a different depth than the mature females. If you start catching all females, you might try setting your traps in deeper water.

Approaching The Float Line
Many neophyte crabbers get into difficulties when approaching their crab float lines, especially in a strong tide or during windy weather. Unless one is very careful, it is easy to get the float line tangled around the propeller.

The propeller may sever the line completely, with the result that the trap is gone forever unless you have a scuba-diving friend to retrieve it. (You might successfully recover such a trap using a grappling hook, but it is extremely difficult to drag the hook in exactly the right spot, even with very precise location markers.)

If the float line becomes fouled in the propeller, it can be difficult to remove. With an outboard or inboard/outboard it is possible to raise the engine or outdrive unit and reach down to work out the tangle. However, this is an awkward and frustrating task, especially in cold or windy weather.

I remember one recent experience where we rushed back to get our crab traps after a day-long fishing expedition. It was just getting dusk as we approached the traps, and a careless manoeuvre resulted in the line wrapping tightly around the outdrive propeller. We struggled for fifteen minutes in the gathering darkness until, fortunately, we untangled the mess, retrieved the trap and found our way home before it became pitch black.

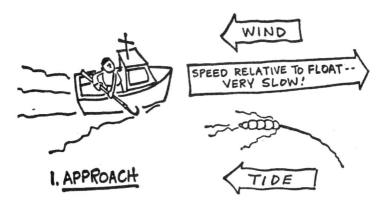

WIND

SPEED RELATIVE TO FLOAT-- VERY SLOW!

I. APPROACH

TIDE

The proper procedure when picking up trap floats is always to approach the buoy against the tide and wind, which gives you maximum control of your boat. If you approach with the tide or wind behind the boat you could sweep over the float line before reversing the engine.

2. GRAB FLOAT
3. ENGINE IN NEUTRAL
4. HAUL IN LINE & TRAP
WIND
TIDE

As your boat gets close to the float, put the engine into neutral and allow the boat to drift the last few feet to the trap. This will assure that the propeller will not be turning if you accidentally bump into the line.

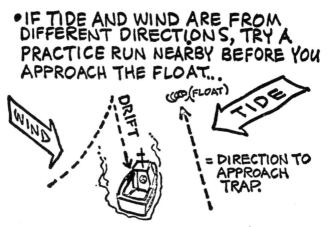

• IF TIDE AND WIND ARE FROM DIFFERENT DIRECTIONS, TRY A PRACTICE RUN NEARBY BEFORE YOU APPROACH THE FLOAT...

WIND
DRIFT
(FLOAT)
TIDE
= DIRECTION TO APPROACH TRAP.

COME TO A DEAD STOP AND SEE WHICH HAS MOST EFFECT ON BOAT --AND HOW YOU DRIFT. APPROACH THE TRAP ACCORDINGLY.

Try to pull the trap so that the line does not lead back toward the propeller. This is not always possible in certain tide and wind conditions, but if the engine is in neutral while you pull the trap you should have little difficulty.

It is a good idea to pull the trap up to the gunwale and let it drain over the side before bringing it aboard. This will minimize the amount of sea water, bits of bait and seaweed brought onto the cockpit floor.

A gaff hook or boat hook is a handy tool for grabbing hold of a float line. Put the hook under the float and twist to keep the line from slipping off the hook while it is being lifted. Some crabbers tie a large ring on the line above their float to make a handy grip.

Commercial Test Results

An interview with the operator of a commercial crab boat brought out some interesting ideas. His observations of crabbing results under various conditions led him to the following conclusions:

1. Large crabs will chase small ones out of the trap. Commercial traps must have an escape hole for undersized crabs. This operator found that most traps, especially after an overnight set, would have either large crabs or small ones but seldom a mixture of both. He felt also that an escape hole helps catch bigger crabs because when a large crab arrives, the small ones leave quickly, making room for more large crabs.

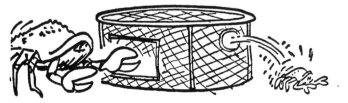

2. He found that long sets were much more productive than short sets. Apparently crabs are attracted to a trap by seeing other crabs already inside, even if the bait is gone.

3. A large amount of bait in each trap catches more crabs than the same trap with a smaller bait.

    During an experiment, some forty traps were set out overnight with only a small bait in each. The crabs were removed and the traps rebaited, this time with five times as much bait in each trap.

The results were startling. The catch per trap was over six times as great as with the smaller baits. While this short test is not conclusive, it confirms other observations that indicate quantity of bait plays an important role in large catches.

A Tip For A Cleaner Boat

Pulling a crab trap into the boat can be a messy experience. Lettuce weed and eel grass often cling to the mesh as the dripping trap is lifted over the side and onto the deck. Bits of loose bait, tiny spider crabs, and sea water fall out of the trap and run into cracks and corners of the boat. This can be very difficult to clean up.

Some large boats have a davit or a platform hinged over the side that allows you to clean the trap outside the gunwale. This works pretty well but is expensive to install and it can be awkward reaching over the side to get at the trap.

My own solution was to buy a children's round plastic wading pool—just large enough to hold a crab trap. Before pulling the traps, I place the pool on the deck. The trap is placed inside the pool and all the water and debris is contained for easy disposal.

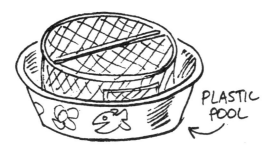

PLASTIC
POOL

Removing The Catch

After pulling the trap into the boat, open the lid of the trap and shake the crabs out into the boat bottom or wading pool if you have it. (Watch out if anyone has bare feet!) You can also reach into the trap and remove the crabs by hand, but this is often difficult since the crab will grab on to the netting or try to squeeze into some inaccessible corner. You might also get nipped if you reach your hand into some restricted space attempting to grab the crab.

If a crab grasps the netting, it is better not to engage in a tug of war with him. If you relax your grip or let go entirely, the crab will usually release his grip and you can grab him and jerk him out of the trap in one quick motion.

Handling Crabs

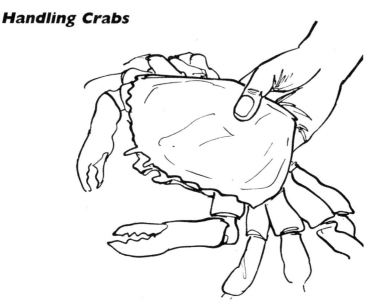

Hold a crab by the rear legs and keep it upright to prevent it from pinching you, or grasp the shell from the rear between your thumb and fingers. It will then have a very difficult time getting its claw around to pinch you, but you should remain alert for the exceptionally agile specimen! Crabs have considerable strength in their claws and have been known to break the finger of a careless crabber. Cans of crabs used as bait in commercial traps are often crushed into grotesque shapes by hungry crabs.

Females And Soft Shelled Crabs

Female and undersized crabs should be returned to the water immediately and the legal-sized male crabs should be placed in a bucket or in a shaded spot in the boat.

Size limits for crabs vary in different areas and you should check local regulations before starting on your crabbing trip.

Male   Female

Female crabs are easily distinguished from the underside by the broad spacing between the two rows of legs. (Remember that "females have a broad bottom." See photo on back cover.)

Storing The Catch

Crabs can be stored in a wet burlap sack, a plastic garbage can or bucket or even in the fish box. They should be kept wet and out of direct sun if possible.

Crabs can live for some time out of water if their gill membranes remain moist. However, they will die very quickly if left in the hot sun or in a drying wind. They will also die very quickly if left on their backs out of the water and exposed to sunlight.

My own practice is to place the crabs in a large plastic garbage can and cover it with wet newspaper or a wet burlap sack. If I plan to keep the crabs for some time before cleaning, I will fill the garbage can with sea water and change it every few hours during the heat of the day.

What Is A Good Catch?

Crabbers are very similar to fishers in their tendency to exaggerate the size of their crab catches. Many persons have insisted to me that they regularly catch crabs over twelve inches (thirty centimetres) across the back and others say their crab catches average nine or ten inches (twenty-three to twenty-five centimeteres).

Unless they have found a whole new race of Super Crabs, their imagination has taken over from the facts.

Most of the legal crabs I catch are about seven inches (eighteen centimetres) across the back with the occasional specimen up to eight inches (twenty centimetres) measured across the widest points of the back.

Samplings by Canada's Department of Fisheries show the average size of legal males in southern British Columbia to be about seven inches (eighteen centimetres) across the widest part of the shell. Crabs from the Queen Charlotte Islands average somewhat larger and specimens in excess of nine inches (twenty-three centimetres) have been recorded. Washington State Department of Fisheries examined over 10,000 commercial crabs and found only two that exceeded eight inches (twenty centimetres) in width when measured immediately at the widest point of the shell. The average was just under seven inches (eighteen centimetres).

Consider yourself fortunate if you have a nice catch of seven-inch crabs. An eight-incher is a real trophy crab!

A convenient method of checking your catch is to cut out a crab gauge from a piece of plywood with the inside measurement just at the legal size. Each crab can then be measured quickly. If it is wider than the gauge, toss it into the pot!

Effects Of Pollution

Crabs are not nearly as affected by pollution as are the various shellfish such as oysters, clams, mussels, etc.

When eating these shellfish you eat the entire animal including its internal organs. Polluted materials consumed by the animal may still be located in its digestive tract. In some shellfish this toxic material tends to build up.

You do not eat the stomach of a crab but only the meat from the muscular part of the body. However, dioxin spills from pulp mills have resulted in some areas of the B.C. coast being closed to crab fishing. Before crabbing in unfamiliar waters check with local authorities and fishing guides for information on polluted waters that affect crabs and other shellfish (see page 62).

I get several calls every time there is a "red tide" warning along my local coast. Persons have read the warnings against taking shellfish and are concerned that this includes crabs. Crabs are crustaceans! While I will eat crabs during red tide conditions, readers should seek independent advice from authorities in their jurisdiction.

Cleaning And Cooking

The time-honoured method of cooking crabs is to plunge them alive in boiling sea water and cook them for fifteen minutes after the water returns to a boil. This requires a large pot if you have a good catch.

Another method is becoming more popular and has many advantages. The crab is killed and cleaned before cooking so that only the meat and surrounding shell are cooked. This saves a great deal of space in the cooking pot. I have found that up to three times as many crabs can be cooked in this manner as compared to boiling them in the shell.

This method also cuts down some of the odour from cooking entrails and makes subsequent shelling of the meat less messy. As well, it means squeamish people don't have to feel like cannibals throwing missionaries into the pot. (Yes, it is true that crabs often "squeal" when dropped into boiling water.)

Commercial crab operations boil alive only the crabs they will sell fresh and whole. The retail customer often likes to buy the whole animal. It has an attractive colour after cooking and the shell can be used as a decoration or even to hold the crab meat when serving.

Some customers also feel they are getting fresher crab if they buy it in the shell. This may be true if they buy it direct from a vendor with a cooking pot next to his stand. (This is the situation at colourful Fisherman's Wharf in San Francisco.) But if you buy crab in a supermarket or fish shop, both whole crab and the shelled meat are probably of equal freshness.

The other apparent advantage of buying whole crab is the lower price per pound. You must remember, however, that shell, entrails and other inedible material make up more than half the total weight. You will also have the labour of picking the meat from the shell.

If you have caught your own crab, the "clean first" method is far more efficient. I learned this method originally from watching commercial crab pickers on the Oregon coast many years ago. I copied their style and recommended it in previous editions of this book.

In gathering information for this revised and expanded book, I discovered what seems to me an even faster and easier way to clean crabs.

(SHOVEL)

Prop up a shovel or other narrow edged tool to use as a striking surface. If you have a large barrel or garbage can, place the shovel, handle down, in the barrel. This will hold the sharp edge up vertically and will also catch the shell and entrails as they fall away when the crab is killed.

Grasp the crab by the four back legs as shown in the diagram. Freshly caught crabs will be very lively and will fight back vigorously, so handle them like a porcupine makes love (...very carefully). If you leave the crabs out of water under a wet sack, they will become lethargic after an hour or two and will be easier to handle. (Do not expose them to hot sun or drying wind or they will die quickly.)

Hold the crab an inch or two above the shovel's edge, then crack down sharply, striking the crab's narrow underflap against the shovel. This will break the crab into three pieces. The underside will split along the line of the flap and leave two sections, each containing four legs, a pincer claw, and a knot of body meat. The carapace or top shell will stick to the edge of the shovel or fall away into the barrel.

Some persons watching this procedure for the first time think it is cruel or inhumane, but this is not true. It kills the crab instantly and is better, in my opinion, than dropping the crab alive into boiling water.

Clean away the bits of entrails still clinging to the body sections and the crab is ready for cooking.

Another effective way of cleaning the crab is with a knife or hatchet. Lay the crab on its back and place the knife or hatchet along the flap. Now strike the back of the knife with your fist or a mallet. This blow is a short punch or tapping action, firm enough to break through the undershell but not enough to cut clear through the top shell.

Now grasp one set of legs and twist them away from the shell, bringing the attached body meat with them. Hold the knife with the other hand to keep the crab shell in place. Then switch hands and twist away the other set of legs and body meat.

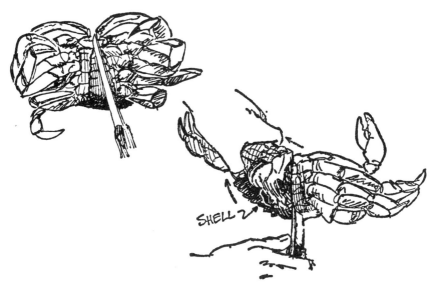

If there is no shovel, suitable knife, or hatchet handy, you can use the method suggested in earlier editions of this book. It is quite satisfactory, but takes a bit more practice to become proficient at holding the crab properly.

Grasp the crab by the upper leg joints and pull them back from the front of the main shell. This will expose the front edge of the shell. Find a protruding object such as the edge of a table or stair, a sharp rock, etc., and strike the front edge of the shell sharply against it.

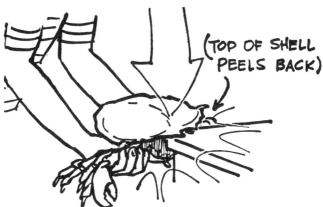

You will find that the shell and much of the crab's entrails will peel away from the legs and body meat much like shelling a walnut.

You then twist the two leg joints together till they snap in half along the front-back centreline of the crab. You can then brush off the clinging chunks of entrails, shell fragments, etc., and you will be left with two crab segments containing four legs and a claw connected to a large pyramid-shaped knot of body meat encased in a thin translucent shell.

Cooking The Crab Meat

These segments can then be cooked in boiling salt water for fifteen minutes. Cook as quickly as possible since raw crab meat deteriorates quickly. It is not necessary to cook the crabs in sea water, but the salt adds flavour. Many persons even add salt to sea water to enhance the flavour of the cooked crab meat.

Others feel cooking the crab in fresh water retains the natural flavour. (I find this quite bland.) They also claim the meat is more tender. Some cook less than fifteen minutes in an attempt to keep the meat tender. This may help but crabs must be cooked at least ten minutes to kill bacteria.

After cooking, the crabs should be soaked for a few minutes in cold water. This cools the shells, which otherwise would continue transmitting heat to the meat, overcooking it and causing it to be dry and tough.

Cooling the crabs immediately after cooking seems to help the meat pull free from the shell and makes subsequent cleaning easier.

Cracking Crabs And Picking The Meat

Picking the meat out of the shell by hand is a long and tedious process involving nut crackers, pointed forks and other instruments to separate meat from the shell.

Commercial operators have evolved several methods to speed up the process. These techniques work on the principle that crab meat (or muscle) consists of fibers that run basically parallel to the long axis of the shells. If the ends of the shells can be opened up, the meat can be shaken or knocked out the opening.

The body meat is easiest to clean. It is encased only in a light, translucent shell that is quick to open. You can press the whole body cavity section (for half a crab) under the butt of your open hand, cracking the shell and opening up the segments of meat. Bits of shell on the edge of the body section can be cleaned away and the section is ready for cleaning.

PLACE LEG SEGMENT (LEGS & CLAW), BOTTOM-SIDE UP, ON A HARD SUR- FACE AND CRACK BODY MEAT SHELL WITH HEEL OF HAND...

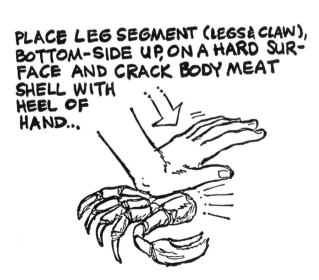

The whole body segment can be cleaned at once or broken up into four segments. If it is cleaned whole, grasp the legs and strike the body end of the legs against the edge of a pan or bowl. This should be a short, shaking motion, and the crab meat should pop out of the body shell when it bumps the edge of the pan.

Do not use a swinging motion (like hammering a nail) or you are likely to have crabmeat all over the walls. The meat often comes loose but doesn't quite fall out. If you move up vigorously for the next blow, the meat is very likely to fly out on the upswing.

Alternatively, break off each leg (with its attached cluster of meat and shell) and shake out the body meat. This may take slightly longer but is easy to learn and very effective.

Cleaning the legs is done in a similar manner. The body end of the leg shell is broken away and the lower joints are twisted off. (There is some meat in these joints, but commercial operations don't feel it is worth the trouble to get it out.)

TWIST OFF LEG (AND PART OF BODY MEAT SEGMENT)...

TAP EACH LEG ON EDGE OF BOWL TO DISLODGE MEAT FROM BODY SEGMENT...

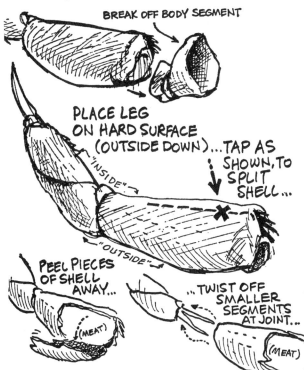

BREAK OFF BODY SEGMENT

PLACE LEG ON HARD SURFACE (OUTSIDE DOWN)...TAP AS SHOWN, TO SPLIT SHELL...

"INSIDE"

"OUTSIDE"

PEEL PIECES OF SHELL AWAY...

(MEAT)

..TWIST OFF SMALLER SEGMENTS AT JOINT...

(MEAT)

Hold the main leg segment (with the open end down) between your thumb and forefinger and bump the side of your hand against the pan. The leg meat should pop out in one delicious chunk.

HOLD SEGMENT AS SHOWN. TAP HEEL OF HAND ON EDGE OF BOWL TO DISLODGE MEAT.

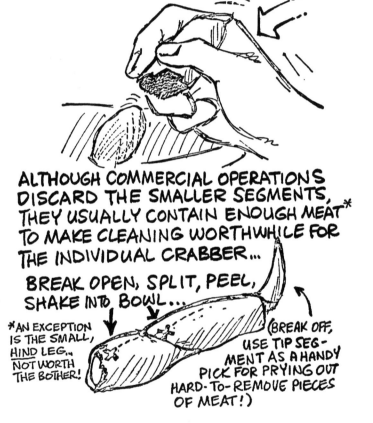

ALTHOUGH COMMERCIAL OPERATIONS DISCARD THE SMALLER SEGMENTS, THEY USUALLY CONTAIN ENOUGH MEAT* TO MAKE CLEANING WORTHWHILE FOR THE INDIVIDUAL CRABBER...

BREAK OPEN, SPLIT, PEEL, SHAKE INTO BOWL...

*AN EXCEPTION IS THE SMALL, HIND LEG... NOT WORTH THE BOTHER!

(BREAK OFF, USE TIP SEGMENT AS A HANDY PICK FOR PRYING OUT HARD-TO-REMOVE PIECES OF MEAT!)

The last portion to be cleaned is the pincer claw. Its different shape requires another procedure. The triangular cross-section of the upper segment can be cleaned easily.

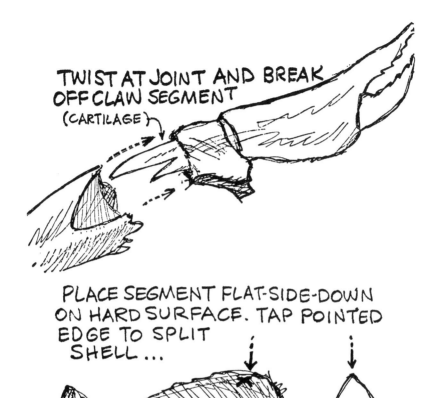

TWIST AT JOINT AND BREAK
OFF CLAW SEGMENT
(CARTILAGE)

PLACE SEGMENT FLAT-SIDE-DOWN
ON HARD SURFACE. TAP POINTED
EDGE TO SPLIT
SHELL ...

(SIDE VIEW)

PEEL AWAY END OF SHELL,
SHAKE MEAT OUT, AS WITH
LEG SEGMENTS.

Twist off the movable section of the pincer, pulling out the internal cartilage connected to it.

Now lay the "elbow" segment and pincer segment on a flat surface and break open the shell in each segment as shown in the drawing. Shake out the meat and the whole crab is cleaned.

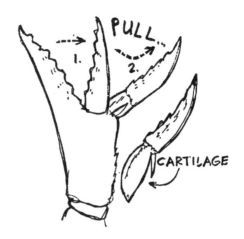

PULL

1.

2.

CARTILAGE

BREAK OFF
CLAW TIP...

BREAK OFF "SPUR",
PEEL AWAY LOOSE SHELL...

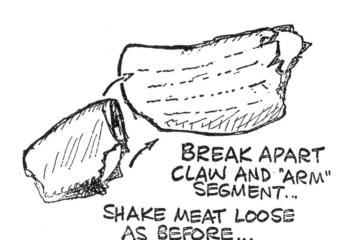

BREAK APART
CLAW AND "ARM"
SEGMENT...
SHAKE MEAT LOOSE
AS BEFORE...

Keep the meat chilled and well covered or wrapped to prevent it from drying out. Eat it as soon as possible. All seafood deteriorates quickly, but crab meat goes downhill very fast.

Crab meat can be frozen, but it tends to get rubbery, especially in a home freezer. Commercial freezing plants can flash-freeze crab meat, subjecting it to a high-volume blast of very cold air. This frozen product is much better, but the texture still suffers in comparison with fresh crab meat.

The Payoff

Crabbing is an exciting outdoor sport, but the main object for most boaters is the delicious final product. After all the work described above, you have the satisfaction of seeing a nice pile of fresh, sweet crab meat ready to eat. It is delicious cold in a crab cocktail or salad. It is also the basis of many gourmet treats such as Newburgs, crepes, curries, thermidors and many others.

One of my favourites is a crab soup made up of two cans of tomato soup and one can of split pea soup. The crab is added just as the mixture gets hot, then a good dollop of sherry gives it the final touch. (For more recipes using crab and other seafoods see the Heritage House publication *How to Cook Your Catch*.)

CRABBING AND FISHING REGULATIONS

Do not go fishing or crabbing along the west coast without checking current government regulations.

The *B.C. Tidal Waters Sport Fishing Guide*, published annually by Fisheries and Oceans Canada, is available free of charge at sporting-goods stores, marinas, and similar outlets. The guide contains all current regulations governing sport fishing for salmon, halibut, rockfish, crabs, oysters, and other species.

Current sport-fishing regulations are also available by visiting the following websites.

B.C. Ministry of Water, Land and Air: Fresh Water Regulations Protection
http://www.bcfisheries.gov.bc.ca/rec/fresh/regulations/synopsis.html

Fisheries and Oceans Canada: Salt Water Regulations
http://www-comm.pac.dfo-mpo.gc.ca/pages/sfg/default_e.htm

Alaska Department of Fish and Game
http://www.sf.adfg.state.ak.us/statewide/html/reghome.stm

Washington Department of Fish and Wildlife
http://www.wa.gov/wdfw/fish/regs/fishregs.htm

Oregon Department of Fish and Wildlife
http://www.dfw.state.or.us/

California Fish and Game Commission
http://www.dfg.ca.gov/fg_comm/fishregs.html

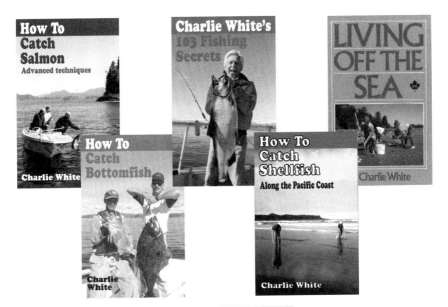

How to Catch Bottomfish

Now in a NEW format, this book is a must-have for families who love to fish. Bottomfish are easier to catch, and they are present year-round. Best of all, they are also an excellent table fish.

ISBN 1-894384-60-1
5 1/2" x 8 1/2" • 128 pages
Softcover • $15.95

The Charlie White library should be basic reading for any fisher, crabber, or shellfish lover on the west coast. Charlie has long been a fan of Nelson Dewey's illustrations, so his books abound with Nelson's amusing cartoons—perfect complements to Charlie's sound advice, good humour, and veteran's wisdom.

How To Catch Shellfish
Along the Pacific Coast

The Pacific coast is a gourmand's seafood playground. Disclosing his latest research, Charlie's practical guide provides all you need to know to gather a shellfish feast.

ISBN 1-895811-49-X
5 1/2" x 8 1/2" • 96 pages
Softcover • $9.95

How to Catch Salmon
Advanced Techniques

The most comprehensive salmon-fishing book available! It covers everything from choosing the right equipment, baits, and lures to how to play and net a fish. Includes a chapter by guest author Jack James of Radiant Lures.

ISBN 1-894384-64-4
5 1/2" x 8 1/2" • 192 pages
Softcover • $16.95

Charlie White's
103 Fishing Secrets

Updated to include more secrets! Charlie shares his tips for improving technique and increasing your catch. This NEW edition includes equipment innovations and the latest findings of Charlie's ongoing research.

ISBN 1-895811-61-9
5 1/2" x 8 1/2" • 144 pages
Softcover • $14.95

Living Off the Sea

This popular guide includes information on how and when to harvest, accessible exotic seafoods, red tide, and even how to live off a beach if stranded. Complementing Nelson Dewey's technical illustrations are fish drawings by Chris Sherwood.

ISBN 1-895811-47-3
5 1/2" x 8 1/2" • 128 pages
Softcover • $11.95

ABOUT THE AUTHOR

Charlie White is an internationally known author, filmmaker, television personality, and fish-behaviour researcher. His books on salmon and marine life have sold more than 500,000 copies, putting him among the top authors on fishing.

Charlie also developed a series of Undersea Gardens marine exhibits in the United States and Canada, which allow viewers to descend beneath sea level to watch sea life in a natural environment.

In 1973, he began experimenting with a remote-controlled underwater television camera to study salmon strike behaviour. His underwater close-ups, in freeze frame and slow motion, revealed for the first time many fascinating new facts about how salmon and other species approach and strike various lures.

He has made three feature-length films about his work, two of which are now marketed on video (*Why Fish Strike* and *In Search of the Ultimate Lure*). He has been recognized in *Who's Who* for his fish-behaviour studies, and he invented a number of popular fishing products, including the Scotty downrigger, Electric Hooksharp, Picture Perfect Lures, and Formula X-10 fish feeding stimulant.

The Charlie White Theatre in Sidney, B.C., which opened in 2002, honours Charlie's contribution to the community. He was also honoured by the University of Victoria as Fisherman of the Year in 2001.

Charlie lives on the waterfront near Sidney, B.C., and continues his unique underwater research on fish strike behaviour. For more information, write to Charlie c/o Heritage House, #108-17665 66A Ave., Surrey, BC, V3S 2A7.